Write Like a ...

Scientist
Doctor
MOVIE DIRECTOR
CHEF
Video Game Designer
GRAPHIC NOVEL CREATOR
AND MORE!

WRITING WORKBOOK FOR CURIOUS AND CREATIVE KIDS

Dedicated to Courtney,
who lifts her people up so high
that they can't help but see
that anything is possible.

Birch Books Publishing
Washington, USA
birchbookspublishing.com

First Edition 2021
ISBN 978-1-948889-05-6

WRITE LIKE A ...

Part One:

SCIENTIST: How to Get Ideas Flowing

VIDEO GAME DESIGNER: How to Create Winning Characters

DOCTOR: How to Find Out What Is Going On inside Your Character

ADVENTURE GUIDE: How to Take Your Characters on a Journey

STAR REPORTER: How to Do Research to Add Real-World Details

GRAPHIC NOVEL CREATOR: How to Make a Storyboard

Part Two:

ESCAPE ROOM! Gather Clues to Unlock the Next Section

MOVIE DIRECTOR: Set the Scene and Paint a Picture with Words

INVENTOR: Start Building Your Story, Test It Out, and See If It Works

CHEF: Clean Up, Trim, and Arrange Your Story into a Delicious Masterpiece

WRITER! Your Amazing Writing Is Polished and Ready to Share

PART ONE

HOW TO USE THIS BOOK

You DO NOT have to be good at writing to enjoy this book! It's about experimenting and having fun. Plus, you're bound to pick up some new writing tricks along the way!

Part One of this book is all about learning and trying out the tricks and tools that authors use to make page-turning, un-put-downable stories.

In Part Two, if you're feeling brave enough to level up, you'll get the chance to build on what you've learned in Part One. You'll gather up the pieces you've already worked on and turn them into a sensational story that YOUR readers won't be able to put down.

By the time you get to the end, finishing this incredible story of yours will be a breeze!

I created this way of writing my name for when I sign books.
I noticed that the S and G both had curves at the top.

To make my autograph stand out, I make those two letters larger and tuck the other letters inside.

Now that you are becoming a writer, you will need an autograph too. What are some interesting features of the letters in your name that you could use to make a unique autograph design?

Practice your new autograph below.

_____ _____ _____

_____ _____ _____

WRITE LIKE A ...

Scientist

HOW IDEAS WORK

It all starts with a great idea for a story.
But what if you don't have one yet?

To get your ideas flowing, let's borrow some tools from science.

The process of writing a story is similar to the scientific method:

1) Ask a question. What should I write about?

2) Gather information. Collect ideas for a character, setting, and events.

3) Make a guess. Choose which details would make a great story.

4) Test it out. Make a rough draft of your new story.

5) Analyze what happened. Review your story draft and see what's working (and what may not be working).

6) Share what you found out. Time to share your story!

In this chapter, we'll focus on #1 and #2. You'll have the chance to practice creating ideas, and you'll have a place to keep the good ones too.

When you **write like a scientist**, you'll experiment, observe, and gather tons of new ideas!

HOW TO MAKE AN IDEA TRAP!

Scan here to see a video version of these instructions.

SUPPLIES:

-4 sheets of blank paper

-Cardboard from an empty box (a cereal box works great!)

-2 pieces of yarn (around 10 inches long each)

TOOLS:

-Scissors

-Hole punch

-Pencil

Create cover art for your Idea Trap in the shape below.

Once you're done, cut it out and paste it onto the cover of your finished Idea Trap.

STEP 1: Fold the sheets of paper in half. Then fold in half again. Then fold in half again. When you unfold the sheets, you should see fold lines that look like this:

STEP 2: Cut along the fold lines, making 32 small sheets of paper.

STEP 3: Take four sheets and punch two holes at the top. Take one of these sheets, and use it as a guide to punch the remaining sheets in the same place.

STEP 4: Use the guide piece to trace two same-sized rectangles onto the cardboard and cut them out. Make sure to trace and punch the holes too!

STEP 5: Put the sheets of paper between the two pieces of cardboard, like a sandwich. Try to line up the holes as best you can.

You are now ready to tie it together. The tips below will help you make an Idea Trap that works like a charm and is easy to use.

PRO TIPS FOR A PERFECT TRAP!

Tip #1 – Line up the holes in your covers and all of the sheets by placing them on the end of a pencil.

Tip #2 – Carefully slip the pencil out while holding your trap with your other hand, and feed the yarn through the hole where the pencil was. Pull it halfway through, but don't tie it yet.

Repeat tips #1 and #2 with the second hole and piece of yarn.

Tip #3 – Lay the pencil along the top of your Idea Trap and between the strands of yarn. Tie each side by making a double knot on top of the pencil. This will help make sure it's not tied too tight.
(Loose is better than tight!)

After tying both sides, slide the pencil out. Your Idea Trap is now ready to use!

Now, whenever you have a new idea, **TRAP iT** here. Don't let any more fantastic ideas get away!

One cool thing about ideas is that the more you practice, the more ideas you can make!

There are three exercises you can do to get your brain ready to start cranking out more ideas:

1) CAPTURE IDEAS – Done! Now that you have made an **Idea Trap**, you are ready to start capturing any new ideas that come up. By paying attention to and trapping your ideas, your brain gets into the habit of forming and remembering them.

2) LOOK AROUND – Surround yourself with things, people, and places that inspire you. Experiences are like food for ideas!

3) PRACTICE! – Each time you practice imagining, creating, and building new ideas, your brain gets better and better at making them.

With the experiments in this chapter, you'll be doing all of these things!

IDEA EXPERIMENT:

Use what you know. Spark ideas from what you have seen, heard, and experienced in YOUR life. Each person is completely unique, so it makes sense that each person's life and the things they experience are unique too. Gather up some of your life details here.

What is the **FUNNIEST** thing that ever happened to you?

_____
_____
_____
_____

What is the **HARDEST** challenge you ever had to face? How did it go?

_____
_____
_____
_____

What is your **FAVORITE** memory, something you like to think about and/or tell people about?

_____
_____
_____

What is your **EARLIEST** memory? How old were you? What were you doing?

_____
_____
_____
_____

IDEA EXPERIMENT:

Just like any good scientist, writers are also good **observers**. By paying attention to the sights, sounds, and events around you, you can gather information that will help you write scenes that are believable.

Pick a place to sit, and **OBSERVE** for several minutes. Use your senses to gather details that will help you describe the scene to someone else. The more information you get, the more your description will help your readers picture the scene, even if they cannot see it for themselves.

WHERE are you? _____

_____

What do you SEE? _____

_____

_____

_____

_____

Now for a challenge! Use your other senses to describe what you observe. Writing with sensory details helps your readers imagine that they are really there too!

What do you HEAR? How would you describe it to a reader?

_____

_____

_____

Pay attention to smells now. Can you tell your reader what the smells remind you of? Maybe something like blooming spring flowers or a smoky fireplace.

_____

_____

_____

Another **FANTASTIC** way to boost your brain's idea-making power is to find and enjoy NEW people, places, and experiences. Some of my favorite things that I have explored lately are pictured below.

Guitar lessons

Animation

Plant-based cooking

What are some things you would like to **explore**? What would you need to learn, do, or find to be able to explore them?

#1 WHAT will you explore?

_____

_____

HOW could you explore it?

_____

_____

_____

#2 WHAT will you explore?

_____

_____

HOW could you explore it?

_____

_____

_____

TIME TO SHAKE THINGS UP!

Think about everything you know about mermaids.
What is a mermaid? A sea-dwelling creature that is part fish, part human.

Now, take what you know about mermaids and

TURN iT UPSiDE DOWN

If you **REIMAGINE** a part-fish, part-human creature, and think about it in a whole new way, it might look something like this ... ⟶

I'LL BET YOU'VE NEVER SEEN A MERMAID LIKE THIS BEFORE!

Now it's your turn! Take a look at the examples from **Greek mythology** below.

Choose one of them to reimagine, and picture it in a new way. Or you can make an all-new combination of your own!

GRIFFIN

Part lion, part eagle.
Usually drawn like this:

CENTAUR

Part man, part horse.
Usually drawn like this:

PEGASUS

Part horse, part bird.
Usually drawn like this:

10

IDEA EXPERIMENT:

Another way to use what you know to make new creations is to retell a classic story and make it your own. You can change the character, change where or when the story takes place, and you can even change what happens.

Here are some examples of classic stories. Pick one of these or another one you know, and change it to make it a new story written by you.

CINDERELLA

This one gets retold a lot!

Humpty Dumpty

Often pictured as an egg, but it never says that in the rhyme. Could he be something else?

ROBIN HOOD

What if Robin was a teenage girl?

What classic story will you use? _____

Now write your version of the story.

_____

_____

_____

_____

_____

_____

_____

_____

_____

_____

_____

_____

A BRIGHT IDEA CAN LIGHT UP YOUR WHOLE STORY

Great work so far! Hopefully, by now your brain feels stretchy, squishy, and ready to pump out new ideas!

Up until now, all of the experiments have been about using things you already know to make new ideas.

In this section, you will start coming up with completely NEW things.

Get ready! The ideas are really going to start flowing now ...

Grab your Idea Trap so you can gather up all of these great ideas you will be getting.

You can do all of the next exercises now, or move on to the next chapter and come back here anytime you need to warm up your brain.

ROLL THE DICE

Not sure what you want to write about? Why not let the dice decide? To do this exercise, you'll need two standard dice.

Below are some things you could write about. If you line them up, they make sense. But if you mix them up, they could make a more interesting and completely original tale.

WHO:
1 – Wizard
2 – Kid
3 – Narwhal
4 – Space alien
5 – Mouse
6 – Robot
7 – Hero
8 – Villain
9 – Monster
10 – Dancer
11 – Veterinarian
12 – Video gamer

WHERE:
1 – Castle
2 – School
3 – Ocean
4 – Outer space
5 – House
6 – Factory
7 – City
8 – Fortress
9 – Fantasy land
10 – Stage
11 – Hospital
12 – Tournament

WHAT:
1 – Using magic
2 – Facing a big test
3 – Fleeing from a predator
4 – Exploring
5 – Running and hiding
6 – Learning new things
7 – Rescue
8 – Good vs. evil
9 – Changing their ways
10 – Big show
11 – Saving a life
12 – Challenging a rival

Roll the two dice, and whatever number comes up, that is **who** you will write about. Then repeat and choose a **where** and **what**. Write a little bit about the combo that you rolled.

_____

_____

_____

_____

_____

_____

_____

_____

_____

_____

WHAT IF?

Flex your new brain waves and answer these what-ifs.

WHAT iF people were pets and animals were their owners?

_____

_____

_____

WHAT iF you could travel to a place just by thinking about it?

_____

_____

_____

_____

WHAT iF time went backward and each day you unlearned something?

_____

_____

_____

_____

WHAT iF you bumped into a person who was **exactly** like you?

_____

_____

_____

_____

IDEA EXPERIMENT: Another exercise that helps challenge the idea-making parts of your brain is solving problems.

Pushing your brain to come up with new solutions stretches the same parts that are used to make new creative ideas.

PROBLEM: There is a pet adoption center on a small island. There are many families on the mainland that want to adopt pets, but there aren't any pets available there. The waters are rough, so travel by boat is not possible. Can you think of a way to bring together the island pets and the mainland families?

Write about how you could solve this problem.

_____

_____

_____

_____

_____

_____

_____

_____

_____

_____

INVENTION

This robot is a top-of-the-line, smart, and powerful champion of modern living.

What is it called?
What does it do?
How does it work?

Write your ideas about this new robot below.

_____

_____

_____

_____

_____

_____

_____

_____

_____

_____

_____

_____

_____

MAGICAL WISH

Imagine you are sitting in front of your birthday cake, waiting for the singing to come to an end. Your best friend has just told you that for your present, they have arranged a magical surprise. For this year only, your birthday wish is **guaranteed** to come true!

You take a deep breath and blow, making sure to get every last candle. What do you wish for?

NEW POWER!

If you could have a superpower, what would it be? How could you use your power in a way no one ever has before?

_____

_____

_____

_____

_____

_____

_____

_____

_____

_____

_____

_____

_____

_____

NEW PLANET DISCOVERED

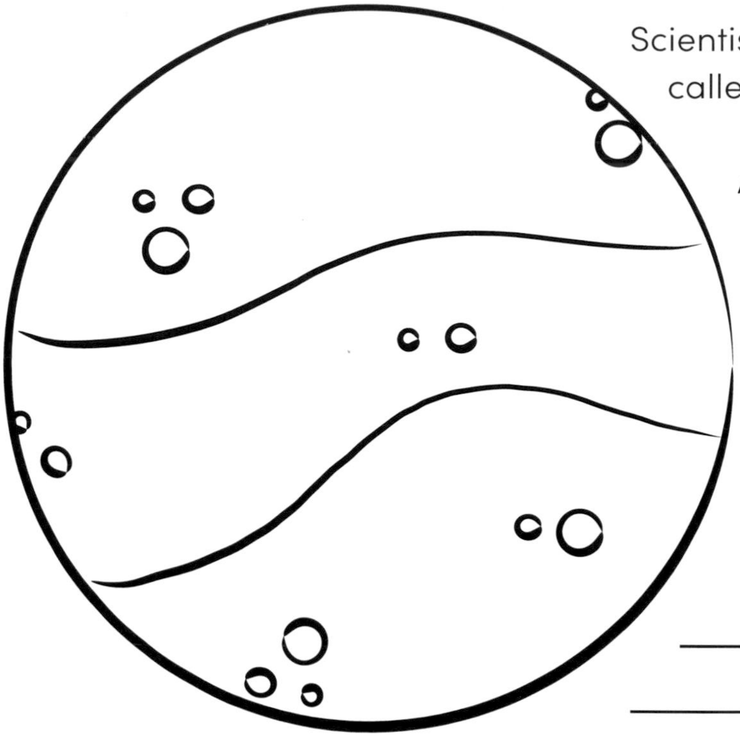

Scientists have just discovered a new planet, called _____ .

As you can see from the beautifully colored picture to the left (hint, hint), it is _____ in color, and its surface is covered with

_____ .

Satellite photographs indicate that there is evidence of life on this planet. It is inhabited by _____

_____

_____ .

Now that you have reviewed the scientific facts, write a short story about a typical day on this new planet.

_____

_____

_____

_____

_____

_____

_____

_____

_____

_____

TAKE IT FROM HERE!

Now that your brain is all warmed up, use your idea "muscles" to finish this story!

The day has finally come. Everyone in town has been talking about it, and you thought you'd never make it this far. You feel excited and nervous (and maybe even a little scared) at the same time. Could this really be happening?

You have practiced and practiced. You know what to do. You check your pocket—yes, it's still there. You have everything you need.

The time is now. You can hear through the window that it has already begun. You take two deep breaths, push open the door, and ...

_____

_____

_____

_____

_____

_____

_____

_____

_____

_____

_____

_____

_____

_____

_____

21

WRITE LIKE A ...

1 = light brown   2 = medium brown   3 = dark brown

4 = light green   5 = medium green   6 = dark green

7 = light red   8 = medium red   9 = dark red

10 = white   11 = light blue   12 = medium blue

CHARACTER DEVELOPMENT

When you play video games and you choose a character to play with, you often select one based on a number of factors. Maybe you want speed or health points. Maybe you want a character that is a higher level and more powerful. Sometimes game characters also come with weaknesses that make them struggle with certain obstacles.

Video game characters are designed to make players become interested in them, care whether they win or lose, and even imagine what it would be like to *be* them.

You can think of story characters in the same way. The more details you create for your character, the more believable, relatable, and lovable you make them.

Write like a video game designer, and detail your character's strengths, skills, and personality. The more time you spend thinking about what your character is really like, the easier it becomes to write what they will say and do in your story.

Don't forget to think about their weaknesses too! These really help readers connect with your character and understand why what is happening to them matters.

What is your favorite video game?

_____

Why do you like it more than other games?

_____

_____

 Thinking about what you like and why you like it can help you discover what you might like to write about too!

Without enough detail, characters seem flat and dull. But when you add outside and inside details about your character, they become more lifelike (and more interesting to read about).

Look at these examples from the classic story **Alice's Adventures in Wonderland** by Lewis Carroll. Can you see the difference when I tell the story with more character details?

1. FEW DETAILS: A girl doesn't like school and then gets lost.

2. OUTSIDE DETAILS: A girl becomes distracted from her homework. She follows a white rabbit far from home and becomes lost in an imaginary world.

3. OUTSIDE AND INSIDE DETAILS: A **curious** girl **abandons her homework** when she spots a funny white rabbit. She **carelessly** chases after him even though she's getting far from home. Before long she becomes lost in a fanciful world where nothing makes sense. **She begins to cry but keeps pushing forward** in search of the rabbit. Finally, she discovers that the only way through this place is to **use what she has learned in school**.

It gets easier to picture Alice as a real girl when I give you more details. In the third example, you can tell what is driving Alice to do what she's doing, how a girl like her will make her way through the story, and even a bit about how she's feeling along the way. Now that's a story I'd like to read!

As you are working on the next few pages, see if you can add the details to take your characters from

FLAT to "I'D LIKE TO READ ABOUT THAT!"

Just like we started the last chapter with what we already know, I'll start character designing with someone I know better than anyone ... myself! If I were to create a character bio (short for *biography*) for me, I would include both inside and outside details. See below.

CHARACTER BiO: SARAH GiLES (PERSON)

I am a person who lives near the mountains in Washington, USA.

Job: storyteller, mom

Hobbies:
paddleboarding
video games
all kinds of art

I'm curious about animation.

Most of the time, you can find me
exploring with my family.

Trusty sidekick: Li'l Ruby the tabby cat

Nemesis (enemy): none (that I know of)

I'm afraid of ticks and leeches (basically, any bugs that stick to you).

Skills and talents: learning how to use new computer programs, listening, coming up with just the right gift to make for friends and family

Special power: I can usually tell what time it is to within 15 minutes without looking at a clock.

Struggle: I have trouble with directions and often get lost when in new places.

Things that I have to watch out for: Video games sometimes distract me when I'm supposed to be doing something else. Also, I reeeally like gummy bears, and if I'm not careful, I'll eat too many.

25

CHARACTER BiO #1: YOU (PERSON)

Fill in the details for a character based on YOU. Include your name and portrait.

I am a _____ who lives _____ .

Job: _____

Hobbies: _____

_____

_____

I'm curious about _____

_____

Most of the time, you can find me

_____

_____

Trusty sidekick: _____

Nemesis (enemy): _____

I'm afraid of _____

_____

Skills and talents: _____

_____

_____

Special power: _____

_____

Struggle: _____

Things that I have to watch out for: _____

_____

Did you know that you can be afraid and still be **brave** at the same time?

Having courage doesn't mean that you don't have fear.

It means that you can push through and try your best even when you feel afraid.

CHARACTER BiO #2: NOT YOU (PERSON)

Fill in the details for a character based on a person, real or imaginary.

I am a _____ who lives _____ .

Draw and write a little about this character. Make it interesting by including some of these:

Job   SKiLLS   Nemesis   HOBBiES   SPECiAL POWER   Fears   SiDEKiCK

_____
_____
_____
_____
_____
_____
_____
_____
_____

There's a game coming up! You can complete all of the remaining character bios or just the ones that you are interested in. To play the game, you will need to complete at least two more bios.

CHARACTER BIO #3: REAL CREATURE

This is for a character based on a real creature, one living now or extinct.

I am a _____ who lives _____ .

The details you would write for a creature may be different from those you would write for a person. Draw and write, including some of these details:

Wants   NEEDS

FEARS   Play

Allies   SKILLS/ INSTINCTS

PREDATOR/ PREY

_____

_____

_____

_____

_____

_____

_____

_____

_____

CHARACTER BIO #4: FICTIONAL CREATURE

This is for a character based on a fictional or fantasy creature. You can choose one you know or dream up something completely new!

I am a _____ who lives _____ .

Your creature may be like an animal or may be like a person. Draw and write, including any of the details that suit your fictional character:

Job
Wants
Needs
Skills
Instincts
Fears
Special power

Play
Hobbies
Sidekick
Allies
Predator/Prey
Nemesis

_____
_____
_____
_____
_____
_____
_____
_____
_____

CHARACTER BIO #5: OBJECT

Fill in the details for a character based on an object that has come to life.

I am a _____ who lives _____ .

Writing about an object as if it were a person or creature automatically gets a reader's imagination going, because it's not something that exists in our daily life.

This is your chance to create funny, scary, or brain-tickling character traits.

There are no wrong answers here, because you are making up something new using your imagination.

What is FUNNY about your character?_____
_____
_____

What is FRIGHTENING about your character?_____
_____
_____

What is SURPRISING about your character?_____
_____
_____

What is ORDINARY about your character?_____
_____
_____

CHARACTER BIO #6: WRITER'S CHOICE

YOU can decide what kind of character to describe. Is there a character that you already like to draw or write about? Get to know them better here!

I am a _____ who lives _____ .

You've learned a few different ways to think and write about a character. Use what you've learned to write about WHOEVER or WHATEVER you want.

Wants   NEEDS
FEARS   Play
Allies   SiDEKiCK
Predator/Prey

CHARACTER BIO #7: WRITER'S CHOICE

Is there anything in your Idea Trap that would make an interesting character?

I am a _____ who lives _____ .

You've learned a few different ways to think and write about a character. Use what you've learned to write about WHOEVER or WHATEVER you want.

Job   Skills/
Nemesis   INSTINCTS
HOBBIES   Fears
SPECIAL POWER

_____
_____
_____
_____
_____
_____
_____
_____
_____
_____

CHARACTER BATTLE!

Time to put your characters head-to-head and see who has what it takes to go the distance and one day star in their own story!

ROUND 1: PEOPLE BATTLE

Shade in the stars below to indicate how each character measures up. Five shaded stars means the character has a lot of that characteristic, and no shaded stars means that they don't have that characteristic at all.

	PERSON #1	PERSON #2
THIS CHARACTER ...		
is unique	☆☆☆☆☆	☆☆☆☆☆
has challenges/ problems to face	☆☆☆☆☆	☆☆☆☆☆
wants something that won't be easy to get	☆☆☆☆☆	☆☆☆☆☆
has powers/skills	☆☆☆☆☆	☆☆☆☆☆
has weaknesses, fears, and/or bad habits	☆☆☆☆☆	☆☆☆☆☆

Now add up the shaded stars. The character with the higher number is likely the one that would be easier to write a story about. If there is a tie, you can flip a coin to decide. Put the winning PERSON in the winner's bracket.

ROUND 2: CREATURE/THING BATTLE:

THIS CHARACTER ...	CHARACTER #3	CHARACTER #4
wants something out of the ordinary for creatures/things of its kind	☆☆☆☆☆	☆☆☆☆☆
has a predator or obstacle to tackle	☆☆☆☆☆	☆☆☆☆☆
has strength/powers/skills	☆☆☆☆☆	☆☆☆☆☆
has flaws or weaknesses compared to other creatures/things	☆☆☆☆☆	☆☆☆☆☆

Now add up the shaded stars. Put the winning CREATURE/THING in the winner's bracket.

WINNER'S BRACKET

```
WINNING PERSON
_____
```

```
WINNING CREATURE/THING
_____
```

To choose the overall champion of the character battle, look at the two characters above. If there is one that you are more excited about or have more ideas for, then they should be the winner. If not, flip that coin.

AND THE MOMENT WE'VE ALL BEEN WAITING FOR ... THE WINNING CHARACTER IS

_____

Now you will leave the action-packed world of video game design and ...

WRITE LIKE A ...

INTERNAL TRAITS

Doctors study science and medicine so that they can diagnose and treat their patients. During a checkup, doctors ask questions and sometimes take a look on the inside to get a better picture of what's going on.

When you **write like a doctor**, you can think about what's going on inside YOUR character.

Here you can see an example of what's going on inside my character, writer **SARAH GILES**.

These things in my brain help me write books.

These feelings in my heart show how I feel when I am writing a book.

And of course, too many gummy bears.

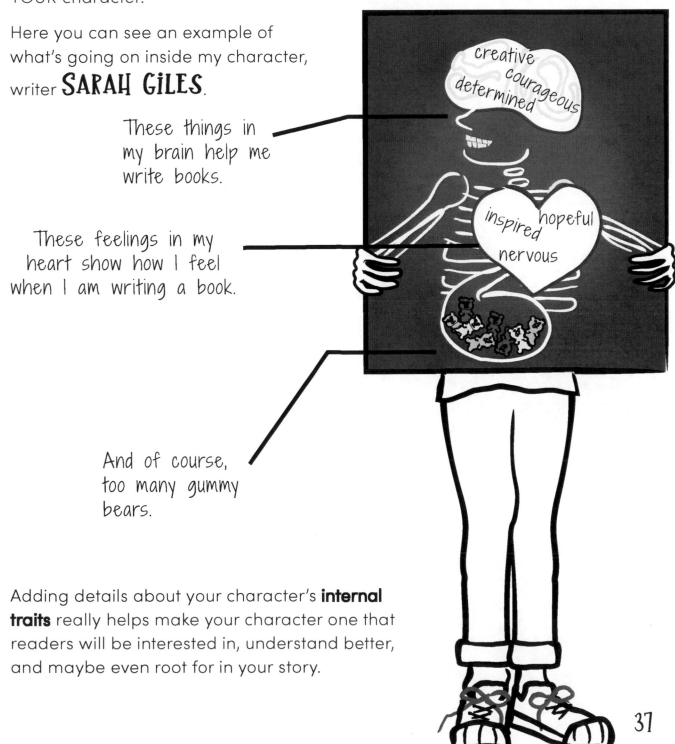

Adding details about your character's **internal traits** really helps make your character one that readers will be interested in, understand better, and maybe even root for in your story.

37

X-RAY YOUR CHARACTER

Now's your chance to think about your winning character and write more about what's going on **inside**. These inside details really help your readers connect with your character and care about what happens to them.

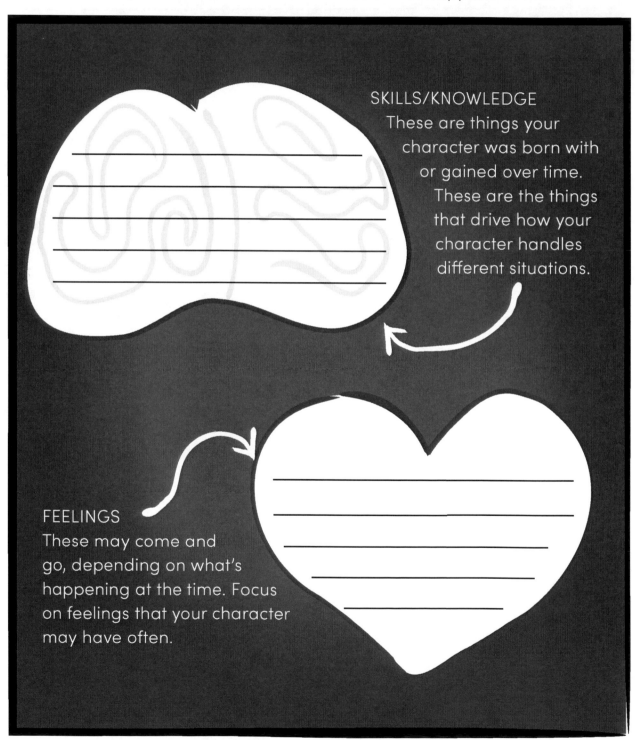

SKILLS/KNOWLEDGE
These are things your character was born with or gained over time. These are the things that drive how your character handles different situations.

FEELINGS
These may come and go, depending on what's happening at the time. Focus on feelings that your character may have often.

EXPRESSIONS

Another way to tell what is going on inside a character is to read their **expression** (what is happening with the parts of their face).

Take a look at the emojis below. What do you think they are feeling? If they were a character in a story, what could be going on right now?

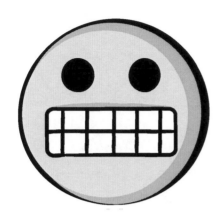

Feeling: _____

What is an example of something that could cause this feeling? _____

_____

What part of the expression did you use to decide?

_____

• •

Feeling: _____

What is an example of something that could cause this feeling? _____

_____

What part of the expression did you use to decide?

_____

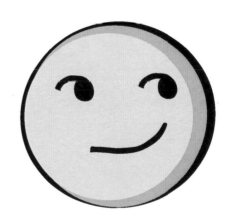

• •

Feeling: _____

What is an example of something that could cause this feeling? _____

_____

What part of the expression did you use to decide?

_____

39

DIAGNOSIS

Just like a doctor checks out the body to figure out what's going on, writers can use **body language** to tell readers what's going on without actually telling them.

Take a look at this pig. Even though he's not speaking, you can probably tell what he's saying with his body language. What is he saying (without actually saying it)?

_____

_____

Here his eyes are the same as the picture above, but his arms have changed. What is he feeling here?

_____

_____

Now his arms are in a similar place as before, but his expression has changed a bit. Look at the expression together with the body position, and name this feeling.

_____

_____

This little piggy's eyes aren't even showing, but I'll bet you can figure out what she's trying to tell you. What do you think?

_____

_____

Body language helps you give clues about how your character is feeling. You can use this trick when you draw or when you write!

40

REVERSE DIAGNOSIS

Can you think of how to describe body position or movements to give readers a clue about how a character is feeling? Draw or write your description of body language for each feeling in the boxes below.

Sad

Excited

Angry

Sick

Embarrassed

Cold

Let's take a break from characters for a bit and ...

WRITE LIKE AN ...

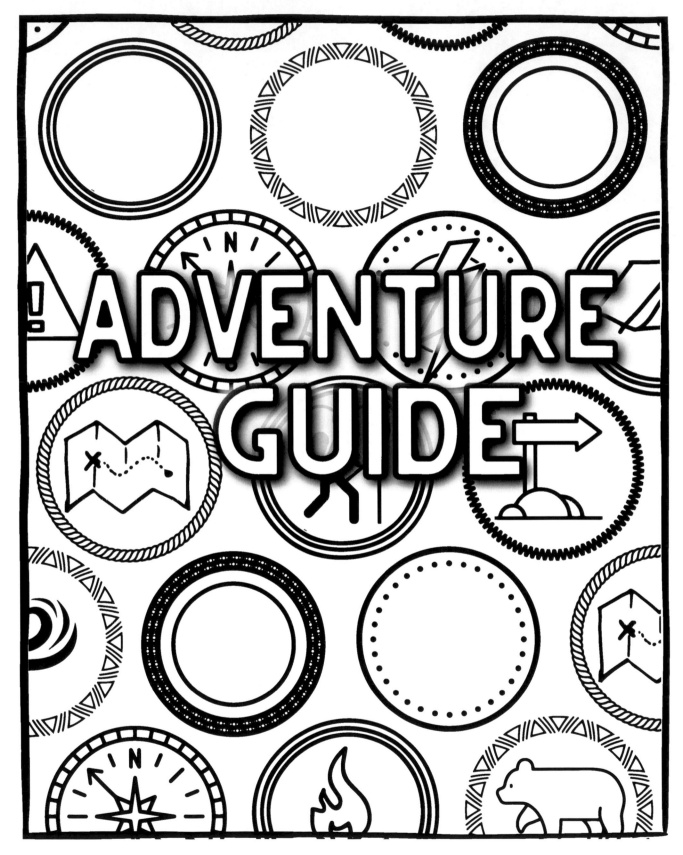

Fill in the empty badges with things you like to see in a story. So far, all of the badges are about adventure. But maybe you like stories about friendship or magic, or maybe you like funny stories. Make badges that reflect what you like.

CHARACTER JOURNEY

Many stories follow a similar pattern, where a character moves through a series of events as they struggle with a problem. It's sort of like going on a journey.

In this journey, a character will face a problem and then decide what to do about it. After they deal with it, readers find out what life is like for the character afterward. Maybe the character has even changed a bit after facing the problem.

This journey is called a **story arc**.

As you work on these next exercises, you will **write like an adventure guide**, leading your readers on this journey (and making sure they don't get lost).

STORY ARC

In this workbook, we'll focus on a simple arc, where a character encounters a problem, the problem gets worse, the character struggles with the problem, and then the character wins or loses.

The arc that you will practice in this book has five main parts:

1) EXPOSITION: This is the first stop on the story arc, where you can set up the scene for the story and introduce the main character.

2) PROBLEM AND RISING ACTION: Just after you begin the story, you can pull readers in by jumping right into the problem they will face. The action builds as the problem gets worse and worse through the unfolding story.

3) CLIMAX: After the action builds, it reaches a point where it's as big and exciting as it can possibly get. At this point, the main character will have no choice but to face the problem and decide what they are going to do about it.

4) FALLING ACTION: The main character has decided what they are going to do about this problem. The writer will detail the character's struggle and will also reveal whether they win or lose.

5) RESOLUTION: The character has faced the problem, and in the ending of the story, the writer can describe what life is like now. Often the main character will have changed in some way, maybe thinking about things differently or doing something that they didn't do before going through this struggle.

In some stories, you might spend more time leading up to the climax, and then the problem gets resolved rather quickly.

In other stories, you might arrive at the climax early on but then spend much of the story detailing the main character's struggle.

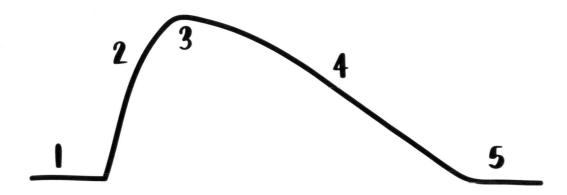

And many stories might have a balance, with almost equal time spent leading up to the climax and detailing what happens afterward.

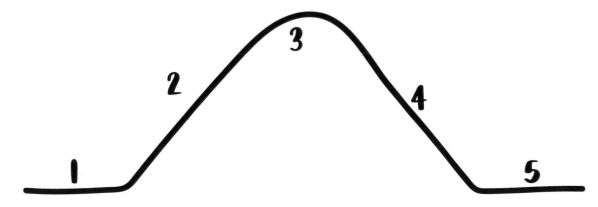

No matter which one you choose, it's important to guide the reader along so they don't get lost. Each up and down should allow your story to still be moving toward the conclusion.

TRANSITIONS

One of the ways you can guide your readers is by helping them get from one event to the next. **Transitions** are like bridges that show how ideas or events are connected to each other. Some examples of transition words are "first," "next," "also," "but," "and so," and one of my favorites, "meanwhile."

Start at the beginning. What words could you use to welcome your reader and tell them when and where the story begins?

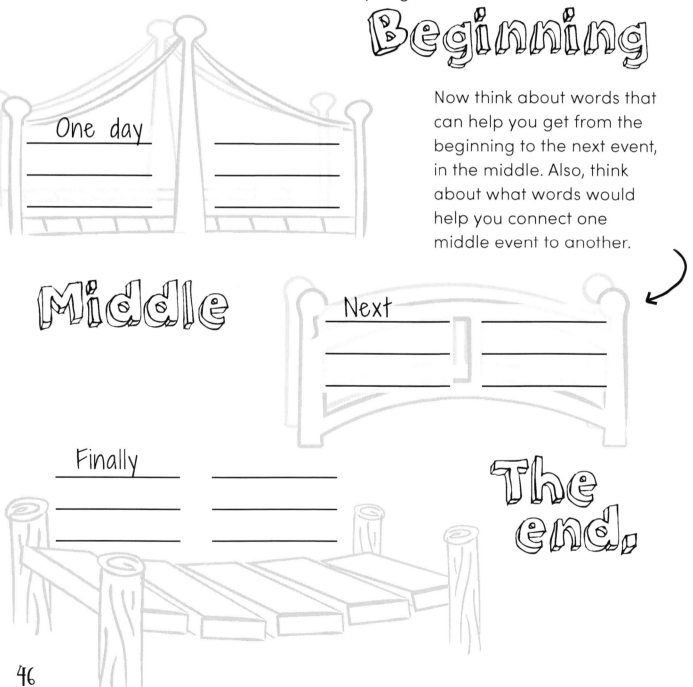

Beginning

One day _____   _____

Now think about words that can help you get from the beginning to the next event, in the middle. Also, think about what words would help you connect one middle event to another.

Middle

Next _____   _____

Finally _____   _____

The end.

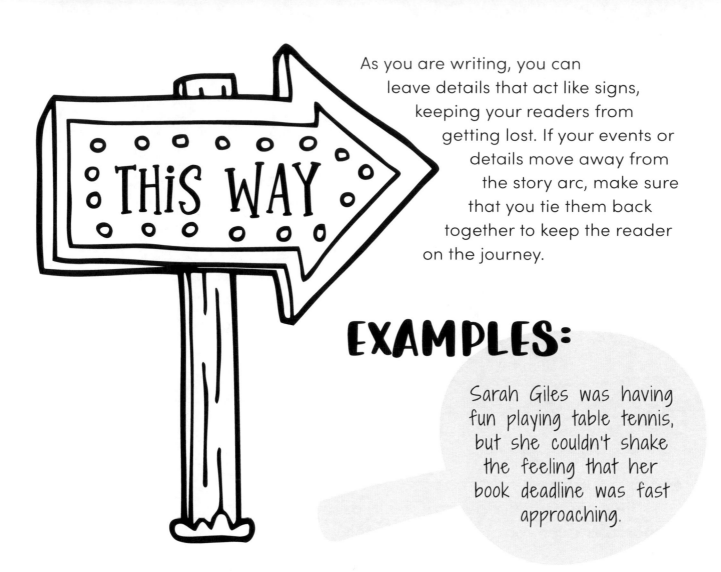

As you are writing, you can leave details that act like signs, keeping your readers from getting lost. If your events or details move away from the story arc, make sure that you tie them back together to keep the reader on the journey.

EXAMPLES:

Sarah Giles was having fun playing table tennis, but she couldn't shake the feeling that her book deadline was fast approaching.

The bear cubs lumbered through the meadow, chasing butterflies and happily munching on blackberries. Food was plentiful now, but with winter coming, they knew they would need to eat up.

Crystal enjoyed her flying lessons, but because there were so few dragons left, she felt the need to be more careful about where she wandered.

TRAIL GUIDE

Writers use certain tricks to amp up the danger, action, and excitement in their stories. Here's a look at how you could use these to keep your readers along for the ride.

Setting a trap for your character somewhere along their journey is a terrific way **to build suspense**.

The trap could be an encounter with a villain, a dangerous land that must be crossed, or maybe a school dance.

A good trap is one that your character **can't avoid** and will really **struggle to escape**.

Some element of **danger** that is **outside the character's control** (or at least, they think so).

It can be obvious danger, like fire or a monster, or it can be hidden. Examples of hidden danger are a run of bad luck or a character that causes trouble for the main character.

GO TiME!

A deadline or event that marks the end of the line for your character acts as a **ticking clock** for your story.

The ticking clock reminds your reader that **trouble is coming** and they had better read on to find out what it is!

Can you spot the action builders that authors have used in classic stories?

The brave girls listed below took on villains, danger, even magic. For years, the suspense in these stories has kept readers on the edge of their seats, cheering for the characters to get through.

*If you have not heard of these stories before, you can check your library or ask an adult, who, like me, may have heard these stories when they were a kid.

What was the trap that Dorothy couldn't escape during her search for the wonderful **Wizard of Oz**?

_____

_____

_____

_____

_____

TRAP

What was the danger that **Little Red Riding Hood** faced?

_____

_____

_____

_____

DANGER

What was the ticking clock that kept **Cinderella** on her toes?

_____

_____

_____

_____

TICKING CLOCK

WRITE LIKE A ...

RESEARCH

To write a nonfiction story or even a believable fiction story, it is important for writers to research the things they want to write about.

This isn't just true for newspapers. The same process works for books, a blog, or even an online video where you provide interesting information for your fans.

When you **write like a star reporter**, you gather facts and information about the people, places, and things you want to write about.

IMPORTANT RESEARCH BASICS

* Do your best to find true facts from **trustworthy sources**. It can be tricky sometimes to tell if something is a fact or someone's opinion, so when you can, try to find more than one person/ organization saying the same thing. If something doesn't seem quite right, or seems too good to be true, do a little digging, and see if you can find another source or two to get to the truth.

* Learn from, but **DON'T COPY, someone else's words**. When you take information that someone else has said or written, make sure to put it in your own words or mark it properly as a direct quote.

* When you use someone else's ideas or research in your writing, make sure to **give your sources proper credit**. Let readers know that your awesome article or story was made with the help of the work of others, and list them by name.

FiND A PRiMARY SOURCE

Have you ever played the telephone game? You start with a few people sitting in a line. The person on the end whispers something to the person sitting next to them. Then that person repeats the same message to the person next to *them*, and on and on.

The more people between the person who first said the message and the person hearing it, the greater the chance that the details get changed or, worse, become something untrue.

When you are researching something, it's best to see if you can trace the information back to the original person who made the discovery. This person is called the **primary source**.

Pretend for a moment that I told you that I read an article from my favorite blog writer about a mayor who was pleased to announce that a scientist in his town had identified a new species of bumblebee.

Now, if you wanted to write a newspaper article about the new bee, who should you try to interview?

Which of these is the primary source of the information?
a) Me   **b)** The blog writer   **c)** The mayor   **d)** The scientist

Sometimes you don't get an answer, but it usually doesn't hurt to ask, and most experts LOVE to talk about the things they are an expert on!

Pretend you are a reporter for your local TV news station. Write a short nonfiction article about a popular event in your town.

Research facts about the event.

1. _____

2. _____

3. _____

Where did you find your facts?
LEVEL UP: put a star next to any facts that you got from a **primary source**.

_____

_____

Now write the article.

_____

_____

_____

_____

_____

_____

_____

_____

_____

_____

_____

_____

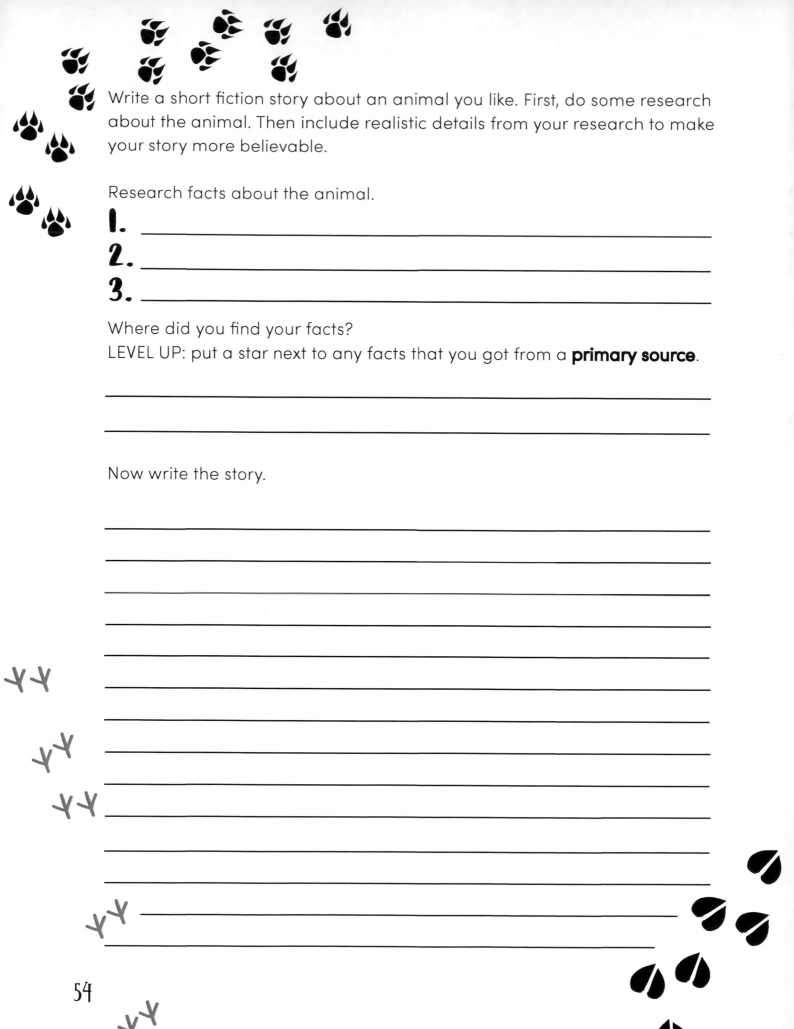

Write a short fiction story about an animal you like. First, do some research about the animal. Then include realistic details from your research to make your story more believable.

Research facts about the animal.

1. _____
2. _____
3. _____

Where did you find your facts?
LEVEL UP: put a star next to any facts that you got from a **primary source**.

_____
_____

Now write the story.

_____
_____
_____
_____
_____
_____
_____
_____
_____
_____
_____
_____

VISUAL STORYTELLING

When you practice **writing like a graphic novel creator**, you are telling your story partly with words, but you are telling just as much (or even more) with illustrations.

You can use the skills you will learn in this section to write a graphic novel, but they are also helpful when planning an illustrated storybook too.

PRACTICE MAKES PROGRESS!

One thing many graphic novel creators have in common is that they draw nearly every day, and they often draw characters over and over and over again. This comes in handy, as graphic novels often require many drawings of characters interacting with each other.

1) Try drawing this taco character on your own:

To build up your drawing muscles, you will need two blank pieces of paper to complete the next steps.

2) Now, take a blank piece of paper and fold it in half. Then fold it in half again. Then fold it in half once more. The fold lines should match the dotted lines on the picture below.

Draw the character, using the fold lines as a guide to get the features in the right place.

3) Grab another blank piece of paper, and trace the character at least three times.

4) Now draw the character again on your own.

Look how much better it is now! You can keep up your practicing using your favorite graphic novel characters next time.

SPEECH BUBBLES

Another thing that sets graphic novels apart from other books is the use of **speech bubbles**. The shape of the bubble is like a code that helps show what is happening.

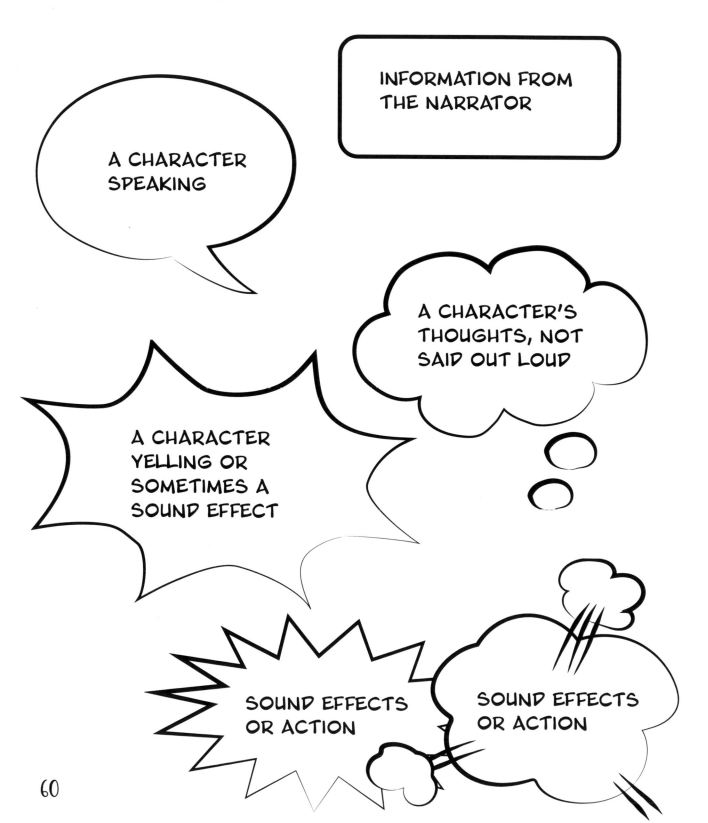

Ready to try it out? Look at the sections of text below and draw a bubble around each to show what kind of writing it is.

HONEY, I WISH YOU WOULDN'T EAT SO MANY VEGETABLES. YOU'LL SPOIL YOUR DESSERT.

HMM ... MAYBE I SHOULDN'T HAVE EATEN THAT LAST PIECE OF BROCCOLI.

MEANWHILE, IN THE LAND OF THE UNEATEN DESSERTS ...

Fill in the speech bubbles, and create a story line for these two characters:

Draw characters to go with the speech bubbles below.

Remember the EXPRESSIONS AND BODY LANGUAGE exercises on pages 39-40? Can you use any of those tricks to show how your characters are feeling?

Now draw a comic strip with two of YOUR characters. You can include dialogue, thoughts, narration, and sound effects if you like.

HOW TO USE PANELS

To use panels, move from one to the other in the same order you would write lines of words in a story. Start at the top left. Travel from left to right. Then move down and start on the left again.

1

2

3

4

When you use a series of illustrated panels to plan out a scene for a book, movie, or other medium, it's called **storyboarding**.

Now that you have some practice with graphic novel basics, use what you've learned to create a storyboard.

For this exercise, try making a storyboard of a shortened version of an old nursery rhyme or fairy tale that you know.

STORYBOARDING PRACTICE

Now, create a scene that could happen to YOUR character.

Come up with a title for a quick story starring your character battle winner. Put the title in panel 1 with whatever artwork you want.

Then storyboard your story idea in the remaining panels. Use as many as you need to tell a short story about your character.

1

2

3

STAY TUNED! SOMETHING **BIG** IS HAPPENING IN THE NEXT SECTION!

PART TWO

*If you have not completed all of the pages in Part One yet, you may want to do those before moving on to the next section.

ESCAPE ROOM!

Before you can go any further in this book, you must gather clues and unlock five locks.

Once you unlock all of the locks, you will have all the pieces you need to write a sensational original story.

HOW IT WORKS

Each of the five locks will ask about things you have worked on earlier in this book. Use what you have learned to collect keys and unlock the locks.

MYSTERY GUEST

To unlock the first lock, you must declare WHO you will write a story about.

The winner of your character battle on page 35 is an excellent choice!

If you want to write about someone or something else, that's OK too, but you may need to do a little extra thinking about them to unlock the other locks.

KEY #1: Character name: _____

What does your character want? _____

What do they have to overcome to get it? _____
(This could be a villain, an obstacle, or a
weakness of their own, for example.)

CHARACTER TRADING CARD

Fill in with details for your character.

Job: _____

Hobbies: _____

_____

_____

Most of the time, you can find me

_____

_____

_____

_____

Trusty sidekick: _____

Nemesis (enemy): _____

Color in a number of shapes to indicate how strong each characteristic is.

Skills and talents: _____

_____

_____

Special power: _____

_____

Weaknesses: _____

_____

Things that I have to watch out for: _____

_____

_____

TELEPORTER

The **beginning** of a story is VERY important when you are writing a book.

Think about what it's like when you are in the library. You can pick up just about any book and check it out for free. And if you don't like it, you can simply get a different one.

But how can you tell if you will like it? Many people read the front and back covers. Others read the first few lines at the beginning of the story. This is an author's chance to grab their attention and pull them into the story.

Imagine that you could teleport to your character and join them at the beginning of a story about them.

Describe what you see and hear, or what is happening at the beginning of your character's story. Think about how you could pull readers in here.

KEY #2: _____

_____
_____
_____
_____
_____
_____
_____

STORY COASTER

#3

KEY #3:

It's time to send your character on an exciting ride. Fill in the stops along the coaster.

MOMENT OF TRUTH

The problem is so big now that your character can't escape. What is happening here?

_____
_____
_____
_____

UH-OH! Now write a problem that your character will face in your story. Think about something that will be tricky, especially for your character.

_____
_____
_____
_____
_____

WIN OR LOSE? What happens when your character faces the problem?

_____
_____
_____
_____
_____

TIME MACHINE

Step into the time machine and discover your character's future! What is life like now that they have faced the problem and won or lost?

Have they changed in any way? Do they have a new habit or way of thinking about things now that they have come through the struggle?

KEY #4: _____

_____

_____

_____

_____

_____

_____

_____

_____

_____

SECRET MESSAGE

Writers create details to let readers know what is happening. But did you know that they often include secret messages to readers too? There are the words on the page, and then there is also what you learn by reading the story.

Maybe you have heard the story of the tortoise and the hare.

The tortoise is quite slow, but he enters the race taking one steady step at a time, determined to keep going.

The hare is a speedy runner, and she's so sure that she will win the race that she goofs off a bit and even takes a nap.

To the crowd's surprise, the tortoise ends up winning while the hare slumbers.

On the surface, this story is about an animal race. But the **secret message** you take away by thinking about how and *why* the events happened is that being speedy is not always better than taking your time and doing your best job.

Now think about the work you did on the story coaster. Think about what message is being revealed as your character struggles and wins or loses.

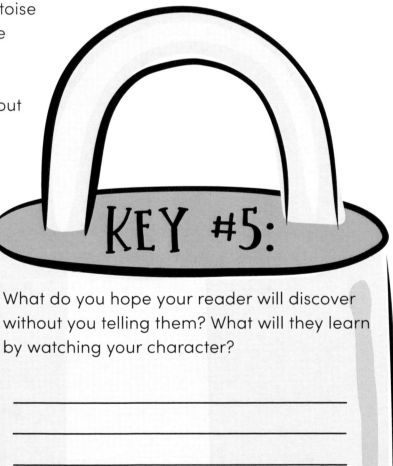

KEY #5:

What do you hope your reader will discover without you telling them? What will they learn by watching your character?

_____

_____

_____

_____

_____

This is a story **outline**. I use something similar whenever I am starting a new book.

In fact, below I have filled in the real-life outline information that I used for my first book, **FITTING OUT: The Friendship Experiment.**

MAIN CHARACTER:

NAME: 10-year-old boy, Max McConk

WANTS: To make new friends FAST!

OBSTACLE: He's super unique and shy, so he is worried about meeting new kids.

BEGINNING: (Actual first lines from the book!) *UGH! This can't be happening! Miguel, my best friend for pretty much my entire life, just moved away! Miguel is my* BRO! *Sure, I have a real brother at home, but that's not the same. BROs are forever!*

MIDDLE (STORY ARC):

Notice the ticking clock!

PROBLEM AND RISING ACTION: School starts in **one month**, and Max is left friendless when Miguel moves away. Max wants to make new friends before school but doesn't know how. He tries a couple of things, but they don't work.

CLIMAX: Max heads to the park and gives it one last try. He meets a new friend-worthy boy who suddenly needs his help.

FALLING ACTION: Max jumps in to save the day. By helping out, he scores a new handful of friends, just in time for school.

ENDING: Max rolls into school with his new friends. He's still the same unique and shy kid, but now he knows that making new friends is possible (and totally worth it).

THEME: Changing yourself to "fit in" isn't the best way to make friends. YOU are unique and special—the one and only you. There are people out there who will make great friends for you based on who YOU really are. And they are not as hard to find as you might think!

YOUR TURN!

Gather your five keys and fill in the outline to unlock the locks.

MAIN CHARACTER:

NAME: _____

WANTS: _____

OBSTACLE: _____

_____

BEGINNING: _____

_____

_____

MIDDLE (STORY ARC):

PROBLEM AND RISING ACTION (UH-OH!): _____

_____

CLIMAX (MOMENT OF TRUTH): _____

_____

FALLING ACTION (WIN OR LOSE?): _____

_____

ENDING: _____

_____

_____

THEME: _____

_____

_____

You now have all the makings of a **FANTASTIC** story! With your carefully planned story outline, you have plotted your

ESCAPE!

Now that you've unlocked all of the locks, you can move forward and ...

Movie Director

SET THE SCENE

The job of a movie director is to make sure that all the pieces of a scene come together. They make sure that the actors, sets, and action bring to life what has been imagined in the script.

When you **write like a movie director**, you can make sure all of the pieces of your story come together in your reader's mind.

Since you have come through the escape room, we are going to start building on the things you have already done.

In this section, you will work on creating **scenes** for your story.

You can use what you know about creating a **story arc** to lay out the main events. Use the senses to make the scenes feel real.

Draw on your experience with storyboarding to think about who is in each scene and why.

Don't forget to let readers know how your character is feeling about all of this!

WORLD-BUILDING

If your story takes place in our familiar world, you do not have to explain much to your reader. But if your story takes place somewhere imaginary, you will want to include some information about how this new world looks, what life is like there, and who lives there. This is called **world-building**.

If you are writing a story that takes place somewhere besides Earth, create some of the details of your world below.

* What is the landscape like?

_____

_____

_____

_____

* Is there magic or special technology here?

_____

_____

_____

_____

* Is there more than one type of creature that lives here, or are all of the inhabitants the same?

_____

_____

_____

_____

MOVIE TRAILER

Think about how a movie trailer gives you a pretty good idea of what the movie will be about, and how it highlights some key scenes.

Look back at what you wrote to leave the escape room. All of the details for your story are there.

Write a short movie-trailer-style summary of what will happen in your story below.

_____

_____

_____

_____

_____

_____

_____

_____

_____

_____

_____

_____

_____

_____

_____

_____

_____

Movie directors make sure all of the pieces of a scene come together. They focus on which characters are in each scene and what's happening. You can do the same thing with scenes of a story.

SCENE ELEMENTS

To keep your reader on the edge of their seat, you'll want to make sure that each scene of your story has all of the important pieces. I'll use the old story of **Pinocchio** as an example.

START

Here's where you can write what is going on in the beginning of each scene.
Example: Pinocchio is alone at night, thinking about being real.

EVENT

What is the big event that will be happening in this scene?
Example: The blue fairy grants Pinocchio's wish, but only under the condition that he behaves.

WHO

Pinocchio, the blue fairy

WHERE

Pinocchio's father's workshop, at night

UP NEXT

Pinocchio goes out into the world and tries to be good.

RISING ACTION

Take a look at key #3 from the escape room on page 78. Take what you wrote for the **rising action**, and set it up on the scene board below.

EVENT

START

WHO

WHERE

UP NEXT

Take a look at key #3 from the escape room on page 78. Take what you wrote for the **climax**, and set it up on the scene board below.

CLIMAX

START

EVENT

WHO

WHERE

UP NEXT

SHOW INSTEAD OF TELL

One of the ways writers make readers feel like they're *really* part of a scene is by *showing* them what's going on, rather than just telling them.

You can use descriptions or drawings of **expressions** and **body language** to help tell what's going on without *actually* telling it.

Think of it like leaving little clues to let your reader figure out how a character feels without you writing the actual feeling words.

Instead of just *telling* you about this trick, I'm going to *show* you! See the examples below.

EXAMPLE #1:

TELL VERSION: Sam was standing by a spider tank. He was scared.

SHOW VERSION: Sam's eyes grew wide when the tarantula turned and started walking toward him. He put his hands in his pockets so no one would see them shaking. He could feel the hairs on his arms stand up as he watched the hairy spider bump up against the thick glass.

EXAMPLE #2:

TELL VERSION: Livvy got a stuffed toy for her birthday. She liked it.

SHOW VERSION: Livvy lifted the lid off the box and pulled up the thin paper that was laid on top. She gasped when she saw what was inside. "Do you think she likes it?" Dad whispered to Mom. Livvy squealed and jumped up and down. She pulled out the stuffed panda and gave it a big squeeze.

Give this a try with your story. Think about how your character might be feeling at the RISING ACTION of your story. How could you **show** their feelings without actually **telling** how they're feeling?

FEELING: _____

HOW WiLL YOU SHOW iT? Write or draw your answer below.

_____

_____

_____

_____

_____

_____

Now think about how your character might be feeling at the CLIMAX of your story.

FEELING:

HOW WiLL YOU SHOW iT? Write or draw your answer below.

_____

_____

_____

_____

_____

_____

FALLING ACTION

Take a look at key #3 from the escape room on page 78. Take what you wrote for the **falling action**, and set it up on the scene board below.

EVENT

START

WHO

WHERE

UP NEXT

Now that you've got your scenes in order, it's time to ...

WRITE LIKE AN ...

DRAFTING

It's time to start putting all of the pieces together to build your AMAZING original story!

It's OK to make mistakes. In fact, mistakes are a normal part of almost all first drafts. Sometimes you have to get the so-so ideas out before you can polish them up into spectacular ideas.

Imagine you are like an **inventor**. You have dreamed up something great. You have carefully thought about and planned the details. Now it's time to build it and see if it works.

In this section, you will focus on putting everything together to see how it fits. And if something isn't quite working, you'll have the chance to fix it later.

INTERNAL AND EXTERNAL TRAITS

Before you start your draft, have a quick checkup with the doctor.

Draw a medical chart of your character from head to toe. Describe any special features, clothing, or tools that are part of your character's **external** appearance.

Go back to your character X-ray on page 38. What **internal** details about your character will help you with your story?

List them again here (and any new ones you think of) so you remember to include them where they might be useful.

SKILLS/KNOWLEDGE
These are things your character was born with or gained over time. These are the things that drive how your character handles different situations.

FEELINGS
These may come and go, depending on what's happening at the time. Focus on feelings that your character may have often.

STRETCH!

You're inventing a new story, which is a big job. But you've already done much of the hard work of figuring out the details.

Now you just need to **stretch** those details (and any new ones you have come up with) into sentences.

Before you start stretching your own ideas, here's a little practice. Look at the example and see if you can stretch each detail into a couple of sentences.

DETAIL: Selena is a superhero who finds lost pets.

STRETCH: Selena Rose seems like any other kid, but at night she becomes Kitra, the cat-loving, crime-fighting supersleuth. Tonight she is on the case of a recent string of petnappings in her neighborhood.

Now YOU give it a try with some things from your story.

DETAIL: What kind of person, creature, or thing is your character?

_____

STRETCH: Now take the detail above and stretch it into sentences.

_____

_____

_____

_____

Now take some of your scene details from your work as a movie director and **STRETCH** them.

DETAIL: Look at page 85. Pick a detail about the rising action of your story.

_____

STRETCH: Now take the detail above and stretch it into sentences.

_____

_____

_____

_____

DETAIL: Now go to page 86. Pick a detail about the climax of your story.

_____

STRETCH: Take the detail above and stretch it into sentences.

_____

_____

_____

_____

Keep stretching details as you turn your ideas into a rough draft!

Mi MAKING ~~MERS~~TAKES IS JUST PART OF TRYING

INSTRUCTIONS FOR BUILDING YOUR STORY

You can begin drafting your story, using all of the skills you have learned and practiced. You can use this checklist to help you remember all of the new tricks you've picked up.

- [ ] *Introduce your character, and let readers know how they are feeling about the events in your story.

- [ ] *Use dialogue and body language to help you show, and not just tell, what's happening.

- [ ] *Use transitions and signs to help your reader follow the events along your story arc without getting lost.

- [ ] *Use sensory descriptions to help paint a picture of your story. These details help the reader feel like they are really there.

- [ ] *Don't be afraid to experiment and take risks. You can create something this world has never seen!

- [ ] *Have fun and don't worry if you make mistakes. We'll get to those later.

Time to build YOUR story!

~~Ruff~~ ROUGH DRAFT

_____

_____

_____

_____

_____

_____

_____

_____

_____

_____

_____

_____

_____

_____

_____

_____

_____

_____

_____

_____

_____

_____

~~Ruff~~ ROUGH DRAFT

~~Ruff~~ ROUGH DRAFT

~~Ruff~~ ROUGH DRAFT

_____

_____

_____

_____

_____

_____

_____

_____

_____

_____

_____

_____

_____

_____

_____

_____

_____

_____

_____

_____

_____

_____

_____

_____

~~Ruff~~ ROUGH DRAFT

~~RUFF~~ ROUGH DRAFT

_____

_____

_____

_____

_____

_____

_____

_____

_____

_____

_____

_____

_____

_____

_____

_____

_____

_____

_____

_____

_____

_____

Nice work! You've got a carefree and creative (and maybe even a little messy) rough draft. To get it ready for readers, you must ...

WRITE LIKE A ...

REVISING

You have all of the ingredients for a fantastic story laid out in front of you. Now you just need to clean, trim, and arrange them into a dazzling, delicious masterpiece!

When you revise, you review your work and make sure you have all the important pieces of a well-written story. But a BIG part of revising is also knowing what to **cut out**.

In this section, you will **revise like a chef** and

CHOP SLASH SWAP & STASH

CHOP!

You've worked hard to come up with lots of juicy details for your character, setting, and events. Details add flavor, interest, and believability to your story.

The downside is that sometimes we end up adding too many extra details to the story. After all, we worked hard to come up with them and don't want them to go to waste, right?

One or two extra details in a story is usually OK, but too many can be confusing. Or worse, they can make it difficult for your reader to follow the character on their journey.

To find out if a detail in your story is "extra," ask yourself these questions:

*DOES iT HELP ME BRiNG READERS THROUGH THE EVENTS iN MY STORY ARC?

*DOES iT HELP ME EXPLAIN WHY THE EVENTS MATTER TO MY CHARACTER?

If the answer to either of these questions is **NO**, it might just be time to ...

Review your story and cut out any extra details. Throw them away, or do what I do, and save them for another story. Many readers love a series!

SLASH!

It's wise to have at least a couple of people read your story and help you revise, but there are many things you can spot on your own too.

Here are some common errors that you can check for yourself.

1. MISSING PUNCTUATION

2. CAPITALIZATION of the word at the beginning of each sentence and proper nouns.

3. SENTENCES THAT ARE TOO LONG OR TOO SHORT

But what is the right length? There really isn't one, but you do want to make sure that every sentence has a subject (usually a noun) and a predicate (the part that contains a verb).

Make sure you have at least one of each of these things in every short sentence.

Next, take a look at your longer sentences. If you have more than one subject and more than one predicate, could you break it up into two smaller sentences? Readers usually like shorter sentences, as long as they each have a subject and a predicate.

4. MISSING WORDS Sometimes, in order to capture what I'm thinking, I write or type so fast that I forget a word or two. Sometimes it's hard to tell what's missing by looking at the piece of writing. But when I try to read the piece out loud, it becomes clear when something is missing.

5. Sometimes I have the opposite problem: EXTRA WORDS. Again, reading the piece out loud makes these jump out at me

Now, check back through your draft. Can you SLASH any extra words or sentences that are too long?

SWAP!

While you are revising, it's a great time to swap out weak or ordinary words and replace them with **synonyms** that are more interesting to read.

Check out the synonym rolls below. Replace the word in the center with something more appealing. (I've already filled in some of my favorites.)

Then check your story, and see if there are any swaps you need to make in your draft.

delightful

GOOD

hair-raising

SCARY

STASH!

Your next exercise is super important to the revising process, but it's also very easy to do!

YOUR NEXT EXERCISE IS TO DO ... NOTHING!

Well, not with your story, anyhow. Play outside, hang with a friend, help a neighbor or your family—do whatever you like to do for fun.

The power of this exercise is to give you a chance to step away. Sometimes I step away from a book I have been working on for a week at a time.

When I come back after a bit and take a look at my work, I am able to see it with a fresh perspective.

I often find mistakes that I didn't notice before. Sometimes there is a spot where I have been stuck, and after a break, I suddenly know exactly how to fix it.

● ●

You have done so much work on your story already. It's a good time for a break.

When you come back to it with fresh eyes, you will be able to finish it up in a snap!

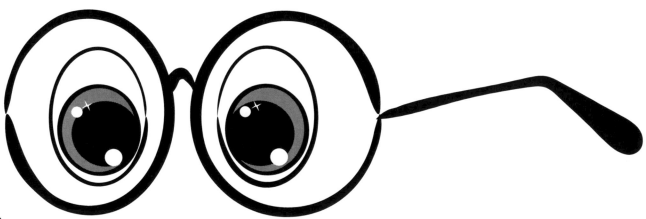

FOOD CRITIC

A food critic is a writer who tastes a chef's dishes and writes an opinion about how good they are.

They write about how the food tastes, how it looks on the plate, and also how it makes them *feel*.

Now be the critic of your draft. Do you have any of these to fix?

*While you are telling your story, are you taking time to SHOW some of the details without telling them too?

*Do your story events bring your reader along the story arc without getting lost?

*Did you include enough details about your character so that the reader feels like they're a part of the story?

ILLUSTRATIONS

When you eat in a restaurant, have you noticed that sometimes there is a special food, flower, or other decoration on the plate with your meal? This is called a garnish, and it is a trick chefs use to make their dishes look more appealing.

Illustrations are like a garnish for your story. By adding interesting and well-placed pictures in your story, you make it even more enjoyable for the reader.

Read back through your draft. Can you spot certain places where you could enhance the story with an illustration?

You can plan them out here and figure out where to put them.

Mark on your rough draft where you will place this drawing in your finished story.

Draw a ♡ in the place where this drawing should go.

Draw a ☆ in the place where this drawing should go.

Draw a ⚡ in the place where this drawing should go.

Draw a ☁ in the place where this drawing should go.

Draw a 🌙 in the place where this drawing should go.

Ahhhhh. Your story looks good enough to eat! The only thing left to do is ...

WRITE LiKE ... YOU! (THE WRITER)

You can decide how to fill this space. Draw a self-portrait, make a collage of your favorite things, or maybe write your name and surround it with drawings about a job you would like to have someday. It's your choice. After all, YOU are the writer!

SHARE YOUR STORY!

Sometimes you write for fun. Sometimes you write for school. And sometimes you write because you have a particular message that you want to share.

Whatever your reason for writing, when you've worked really hard on something and it turns out great, why not share it with friends, family, and of course, your fans?

If you want to turn your finished story into a paper book, scan the QR code below to download a final-draft template. Write or type your final draft on the template and follow the instructions to assemble a finished book.

Get printable final-draft paper plus ideas and instructions for ways you can make your story into a BOOK here.

sarahgilesbooks.com/share-your-story

The next couple of pages will give you a chance to practice and plan some additional ways to polish up your finished book.

COVER ART

Draw your book cover in the space below.

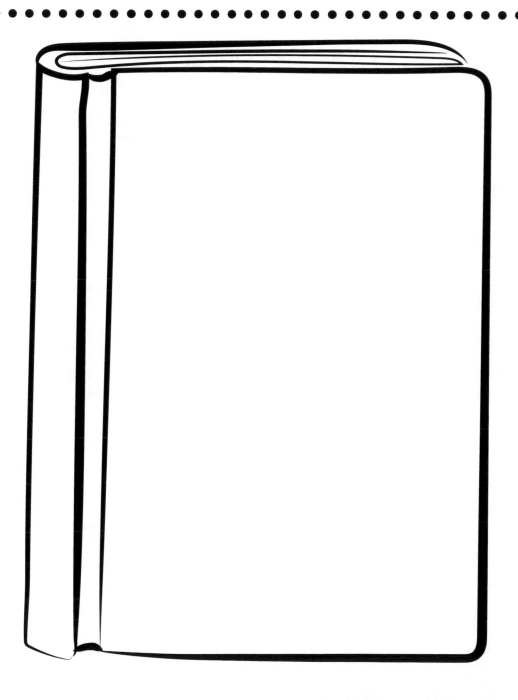

DEDICATION

In this section, you can express your **gratitude** or appreciation to someone who helps you with your writing.

If you have someone in mind, go for it! But if you are stuck, think about choosing one of these: someone who inspired you, someone you want to thank, someone you want to honor, or someone you love.

In this section, you can write who the book is dedicated to, and if you wish, you can write a little bit about why you chose them.

DEDICATED TO

_____

_____

_____

_____

Copyright is the law that protects your ownership of the work that you create. In the United States, you automatically have copyright ownership of your original work the moment you write it. You can label your work so that it is clear who created it and when.

For a book, you can set it up this way:

© _____ **by** _____
     Year   Your name

ABOUT THE AUTHOR

Create a short author biography of yourself to include with your story.

Often these will include where you live and something about your family or pets. I sometimes include a little about my hobbies too.

You can get these and other details from your character bio on page 26.

Don't forget to draw or paste a picture of yourself.

_____

_____

_____

_____

_____

_____

_____

_____

_____

_____

CONGRATULATIONS!

If you have completed your story, turned it into a book, and shared it with readers, you are now, by definition, an **AUTHOR!**

Plenty of folks write stories, and many of them share them too. But not everyone has what it takes to prepare, write, revise, and assemble a book.

Getting to this stage is a HUGE accomplishment!

You now have the tools and tricks of the book-writing trade, plus you've had a chance to practice them using YOUR OWN ideas.

But the **MOST IMPORTANT** thing that you have now is the confidence in knowing that even if it is not fast, even if it is not easy, even if you need to make changes, you **CAN** push through and **WRITE A BOOK!**

THE END

(of this book).

But for you, **THE WRITER**, this is only the beginning!

OTHER BOOKS BY SARAH GILES

FITTING OUT - A bestselling chapter book series, perfect for readers ages 7-10.

10-year-old Max is finding his own way to get through elementary school life, sharing his triumphs, fails, and many laughs along the way.

SWITCHES AND PEEPS – A funny, new early chapter book series, perfect for readers ages 6-8.

"A funny, sweet-natured tale about getting along despite differences." - Kirkus Reviews

Made in United States
North Haven, CT
02 July 2022

20902291R00070